Poetic Elements

Poetic Elements

Words I Never Said

MPJ

ISBN: 0692121293

ISBN-13: 978-0692121290

DEDICATION

Dedicated to the women I once loved. Thank you for the lessons.

CONTENTS

ACKNOWLEDGMENTS

To the women I once loved, still love & will love in the future: Thank you. Thank you for your presence, your essence & the idea of you that has added tremendous value to my life. Thank you to my family and friends who have always believed in & supported me through every version of myself. I thank God for allowing me to see as many sunrises and sunsets as I have thus far, and for placing people in my life over the years who have continuously taught me so much about myself. Finally, I want to thank you for lending me your eyes, ears & hopefully your heart.

Intro

It took years,
blood sweat & tears,
my daydreams and my worst fears
all intertwined in the pages you'll read here.

I've lived dreams I never had &
lived through nightmares I never shared.

I've loved a woman that didn't care &
I've been loved by another, but unaware.

Some scars I don't reveal
because some wounds will never heal.

I spend my nights overthinking &
spend my days writing truths
I never plan on speaking.

Words I Never Said

For so long I've lived inside my head,
often times haunted by the words I never said.
It's too late for me to right the things that I've done wrong,
but if you lend me your ear,
maybe I can write my wrongs
and weave words in such a way that when read,
they reach out and touch your soul
so that you'll come to understand
the depths of a man
who's only trying to be
the very best that he can.

His(s)tory

They say history repeats itself.
If that's the case,
I pray I live long enough to meet myself,
to bestow upon him all the lessons
learned in my younger years,
reminiscing about the future
wondering how did I get here.
So far from where I planned,
so much to explain… How do I make him understand?
The tragic tale of heartbreaks that await the road ahead,
matters of the heart have the ability
to severely change the man,
the man who stands before you was not always as I seem.
Like you, I was once full of life & I believed in everything,
as long as I was a good man anything I could achieve.

Naïve.
The better the man,
the more the world will try to cut you off at the knees.
Still proceed,
the road will be long & at times lonely,
you will have to walk alone with no one by your side,
and no one cheering you on.
You'll learn to accept the rain,
you'll learn to express the pain—
All on the road to becoming the best possible man.
You'll lose hope,
people will walk out on you,
but that doesn't mean the show is over,
you'll gain focus,

a greater understanding & a sense of belonging.

One day you'll see
that things are not always what they appear to be
because history repeats itself.
Since that's the case,
I know you'll live long enough to meet yourself
and bestow upon him all the lessons
learned in your younger years.
Then you'll understand the road that lead you here.

Shards

Reflections of the person I was
in shards of glass all around me.
It's often said that life has a sense of humor.
How ironic is it that at the very moment
I find myself falling apart,
I now see myself in pieces…

Lately

Lately you've been going through the motions,
not dealing with emotion,
losing sleep & focus.
You're broken,
you can't hide it forever,
you know this.
Through all the fake smiles
& unengaging hellos,
I know—
Deep down you're wondering if it shows.

I See You

I see past the facade that your past has created,
the beautiful veil you put on every day
as you leave home like a shield of armor,
the walls you've carefully constructed
over time all around you
to keep people at bay,
because in your mind, if they saw the real you,
they might choose not to stay.

I see you.
I see the pain disguised as a sparkle in your eyes,
the hurt that hides in your smile,
the crying out when asked if you're okay
masked in your response: "I'm fine."
I see you.

I don't own these words,
they are as much mine as they are yours.

Choose YOU

A drop of blood leaves my hand on its way to the floor,
I didn't realize the cut was this deep,
nor did I realize how fast time would pass
from that initial bleed.
My thoughts are becoming scattered now,
so if this should be the last time that we speak,
I need you to remember this about me:
Loving you was the slowest form of suicide,
cutting ties was a desperate attempt to survive,
memories of being in love alone
can no longer reside in my heart,
neither can the fear of being alone,
my past has caused enough tears,
I cut you off because we both couldn't survive here.

In the now & for once…
I choose me.

Turn the Page

Turn the page on your pain,
turn the page on your sorrow.
Like any good book,
the story evolves.
You weren't made to remain the same,
there's power in change,
there's strength in growth.
This chapter of your life has ended,
but the book is far from over...
turn the page.

Still

You can't move on until you've healed,
you can't move forward until you've learned the lesson,
sometimes standing still is a form of progression.
Be still, heart.

Then

Things I never said:
I was young, lost & insecure
I didn't love me
I wasn't capable of loving you.
Everything you said about me was true.
I was a fool
because instead of acknowledging it
I put the blame on you.
Denied every truth, grew old in my ways
at a young age, & hid myself away,
inside every vice you could name.
Let me explain,
you were searching for the real me &
I was busy running from you,
because opening up to you
meant I'd have to face my truth &
the root of my pain.
Which grew into problems
that I couldn't contain,
so I ran away & hid.
You'd never dig deep enough to find me here,
beneath my fears.

Now

I'm older now,
I know who I am,
I love myself & I will always love you.
Everything you think of me isn't true.
Although I'm still a fool
because instead of moving on
I fell in love with the memory of you.
As I've grown older in age
I've changed my ways,
I'm no longer hiding & I've got things to say.
Please bare with me
while I try to explain.
Your love made me the man that I am today,
you've always been the light
guiding my way.
Today is the day that I face my truth,
we've already done in each other's lives
what we were meant to do.
You were meant to build me,
I was meant to break you &
I'm so sorry for all the things
that I put you through.

Closure

Everyone speaks of you
as if they know you personally,
yet no one can show me the way to you,
I'm not even sure what I would say to you,
I've been told I need you in order to move on,
but do we ever truly move on
or
do we just learn how to live within
the broken parts of what used to be a life?
I'm unsure of what comes next,
I understand the need to move forward,
but it seems I've forgotten how to take the first step,
I don't know how to exist within this emptiness

and I'm not entirely convinced
you're anything more than a myth.

Write My Wrongs

I lied to you,
there's no valid reason why,
there was no malice,
just an attempt to hide,
not another woman,
just the soul of a broken man,
the logic of your love
was something I couldn't understand.
How could you see more good in me than I see in myself?
You were a dream come true,
but a dream nonetheless,
and I treated you as such,
knowing full-well someday I would have to wake up.
Yes, I lied to you & there's no valid reason why.

An apology to you, although overdue,
would never do what I intended it to,
but it deserves to be heard.
I just pray you see the heart behind them,
not just letters formed into the words.
I'm sorry.

Disappearing Acts

Disappearing acts.
I leave as if I'm never coming back
just to reappear
unannounced while silently screaming out
that I'm here.
I'm seen
but never clearly,
I keep people close
but never near me.
I walk away hoping that you'll ask me to stay,
I apologize I'm guarded & I can't let it down,
the thought of being vulnerable to someone who might not
stick around is something I could never live down.

I could never live with the fear of giving you my all
and you walking away with it.
A defense mechanism & a psychological prison—
One that I can't escape.

Prison

I've made a lot of bad decisions—
All of them with precision,
though I had good intentions.
These moments I keep reliving,
they have become my prison,
this has become the prism
through which I view the world.

War

Heart versus mind.
When the stars align,
purpose is defined.
It can seem divine,
rarely has this happened to me,
I've always been at war with myself,
evidenced by the scars & welts,
tormented by decisions that I've never forgiven,
constantly balancing who I am
with who the world says I should be.
How does a good man find happiness
in the chaos of today's society?

Society

Society says you'll be more of a man
if you can juggle the number of women
you have on more than one hand.
What happened to chivalry?
Or finding that one woman God made
just for me & trying to build we.
Today's world is one I can't comprehend.
Lost in translation is the true definition of man.
Honesty, loyalty, commitment & trust—
These are more than words for some of us.
The value these words hold make up the sum of us.

5:15

My internal alarm clock
led me to a voice that warmed
the coldest parts of my heart.
What is it that sets her apart?
Made this opposite attract
& her a different reaction…
The unjust laws of attraction.
Love is an undying mystery.
Looking in her eyes always mystified me.
If only mine had caused the same feat,
so everyday
around this time.
I quietly go about the business
of completely shutting down,
drowning out the traffic.

All the sights and sounds,
so I can be alone with the memories
as I slowly watch them die
every day at 5:15.

Goodbye

It's hard to say goodbye to someone you love,
It's even harder to say goodbye to the idea
of who you thought they were.
You fell in love with who you wanted them to be,
in turn you were disappointed by reality,
expectations led you astray,
you broke your own heart,
yet you still chose to stay,
hoping one day they'll live up
to the potential only you had for them,
sadly prolonging your pain.
You can never love someone enough to make them change,
no matter how great the potential for love is.
It'll never be enough to sustain.

It's only so long you can live a lie
before you have to say
goodbye.

I Love You

"I wish you the best"
and just like that,
I've found the most painful way
to say I love you.

It's Over

Your mind knows it's over & it's time to move on,
but you hold on desperately hoping for a sign.
That will never come.
Your heart won't accept the truth:
You fell in love
with someone who doesn't love you.
There's a hurt that comes with that.
Only experience can understand,
you're not alone,
you're not weak,
simply because
in this moment you don't know how to be strong.
Your heart's not wrong.
You'll know when you're ready to move on

when the pain of feeling alone
is worse than the hurt of being alone.

Agony

Love is out of season &
she's out of reasons,
she's done using &
now she doesn't need him.
So she kills him softly
yet she leaves him breathing
dying inside,
but no one can see it.
Now love is one more thing
he doesn't believe in.

Internal demons
leave him forever thinking
that he's still him and
every woman is her.
Love was only a blur.
His pain wasn't meant to be heard,
so he silently screams
without saying a word.

Epiphany

If only a change of scenery
could change what you mean to me,
I'd go away tomorrow
and never return to my sorrow.
But no matter where I'd go,
my memories would follow,
haunting me.

Which brings me to my epiphany
you were a gift to me,
a blessing in disguise,
a lesson I cannot deny.
I can't out run my pain.
Things can't go back to being the same.
Pain requires growth & growth requires change,
not of scenery but of everything I've aimed to be.
So, I'll become who I was born to be.

Father

I understand now,
how much you not being there
shaped who I became.
I lived my life with a blueprint of bad decisions,
consciously making choices to prove that I was different.
I grew up in the shadow of a man
that I didn't fully understand.
Too young to comprehend that he was just human,
with his own conflicts & emotions in the moment.
As a man, I understand now & it's all forgiven.
You walking away,
is the reason I sought out commitment.
Why I loved too hard and stayed too long,
why I put my heart in places
where it didn't belong.

I understand now,
I can no longer live in your shadow,
I can no longer live up to simply not being you.
I must be me,
I must be a King.

The Measure of a Man

The measure of a man is not how he stands
when his feet are firmly planted on flat ground,
but how he stands in the moments
when his world collapses all around him.
They say pride comes before the fall,
but sometimes pride is the thing
that keeps you standing when the ground
crumbles beneath you.
Being a man doesn't mean when things are going right,
I don't need you.
Being a man means even when things are going wrong,
I won't leave you.

Unborn Son

Be a better man than your father.
A message I was never given
but I still tried to receive.

Though at times I fell short
know that at times you will too
and this is ok,
this is just what humans do.

But after every fall you must stand,
rise to as many occasions as you can
don't let the moment pass you.
Moments make up your memories, whether they're good or
bad.

Be a better man than your father.

Learn from your mistakes
but don't live in them,
forgive yourself.

Know that love & loss go hand-in-hand
and I pray you experience both,
as both will help to build the character of a man.

It's ok to be hurt, don't be ashamed
there's not a man alive that doesn't feel pain.
Just don't let the pain of being hurt
turn you into what hurt you.

Be a better man than your father.

You may not understand now
but one day you will
and know that when you do,
even if I've moved on from this world
these words will still be here.

May they forever guide you
to your best decisions &
if you should lose yourself along the journey
may they help you find your way.

I can't tell you who you are,
only what I hope you'll be.
And if there ever comes a time
when you no longer remember me,
know your father was a good man
but please son

Be a better man than me.

Rise

A relationship ending doesn't mean you're finished,
it means you're overdue for a new beginning.
People change just like seasons do.
So, you fell for a warm lie instead of the cold truth.
Life knocked you down, but now it's time to rise.
Everything happens for a reason.
Although it won't lessen the pain,
the lessons learned through your tears
will help you find meaning,
so take the night,
cry it out
in the morning rise—
Rise without a single doubt.

Ashes

Out of the ashes of my past,
my future was born anew.
My first breath of life
was the very sight of you.

Searching for You

I've searched for you
in every woman that I ever knew,
dreamed of a love
unconditional & true,
looked in a thousand eyes
trying to find a glimpse of you,
I've searched high & low,
over & under.
I've aimed for the skies
and settled in sewers—
All in an effort to find you,
a soul that vibrates
the same frequency as mine,
an intelligent spirit & a beautiful mind.

Yes,
I've searched for you
in every woman that I ever knew.

Soul Mate

I don't talk much but my soul speaks daily,
you'll only comprehend if we're on the same wavelength.
Few understand the energy that lies within.
When a touch won't do & words won't suffice,
my soul speaks in seek of a connection
I've searched for my whole life.
My better half of my best self,
equals a greater whole than I could
ever know on my own.
She's what dreams are made of &
I'm the man she was made for.

I stared down my demons
to be right for her.
Destroyed the darkness within me
to be a light for her.
All in an effort to spend my life with her.
I've already earned her hand,
our souls have already spoken
as this was already planned.
The simple thought of her,
has already made me a better man.

Beautiful

You're beautiful
with no illusions
inside & out,
so there's no confusion,
from the depth of your eyes,
to the way your cheeks perfectly curve into your smile
before hearing the softness of your voice,
spoken with such southern hospitality,
only to be out done by an equally charming personality.

You astound me.
Unbelievable yet authentic,
unexplainable yet simplistic enough
to be perfectly described as amazing.

Yet still this word doesn't emphasize enough
what I see when I see you,
so this is me hoping you see
through me what I see in you.

Thank you for being today's muse;
I wrote this just for you.

Marry Me

In my mind,
my heart,
my soul & my spirit,
I'll love you endlessly
until love itself ceases to be.
That's what it means when I say I love you,
that's the reason I put
no one but God above you.
I see you in every one of my empty stares,
thoughts of you are behind every lost train of thought.
When we're apart,
I'm lost in the confusion created by your absence,
completely addicted to your whereabouts.

Wandering around until you return with my purpose in
tow, my heart is yours if you didn't already know,
I'm in love with you if it doesn't already show,
I've thought long & hard about this thing called life.
The one thing I know for certain:
I want you to be my wife.

Diamond

The stress the world caused couldn't faze her
because pressure was what made her.
She was a diamond with rare gems hidden within.

Queen

The ease at which you carry yourself
along with the weight of this world—
This world that, at every turn,
tries to limit, control, or define you—
I'm in awe of your stride,
the way you maneuver the corridors in a world
that's intent on keeping you in places
your heart, mind & spirit can't reside.

What I feel for you can't be described.
You are the missing piece,
the unbroken link
to the past, present & future
of a world that rarely deserves your presence.

You are the very essence
of living proof that God exists,
so wear your crown & never hold your head down,
know your worth & speak your truth.
You are invaluable simply because you're you.

Switch

Some people can flip a switch,
I never had this gift.
In an instant
you went from something I looked forward to,
to something I could only reminisce.
Now you've moved on &
I'm trying to paint the most vivid picture of being strong.

This is the difference between love & like,
one moves on,
the other dies a thousand deaths
reliving the relationships final steps.

Love

Love changes everything.
You see,
"like" stalls.
Love was always meant to evolve
everyone that it involves.
We stand alone until we fall
for one we can't stand to fall asleep without,
someone who erases all doubt.

Love Letters

Writing love letters with invisible ink,
I pour my heart onto these pages—
You don't even blink.

Change

Things change,
dreams fade,
situations change
drastically like the transition from night to day.
We fantasize the future
& romanticize the past,
when the truth is:
Today is all we truly ever have,
so live in your moments
because the sun sets much too fast—
And regrets…
regrets can be everlasting.

Poetic Elements: Words I Never Said

My World

When I was young I dreamed of seeing the world
then I saw you,
thank God for making dreams come true.

51

ILYETLYG

I can't remember a time when I didn't
Love you more than words could describe.
You were always the one, always
Enough to make me see things clearly,
To make me understand the value of love, so
Let me make this clear to
You: I'll never leave & I don't want you to
Go, but I understand if leaving me sets you free &

*The last line of this poem is all the bolded words read
from top to bottom*

Another Life

In another life
you'd be mine & I'd be yours.
There would be more between us,
than these empty words & forgotten smiles.
I once saw heaven in your eyes &
now I'm wondering what could I have done
to deserve a life
without you...

I Miss You

I miss you.
Even more than I miss you,
I miss the people we would have grown into.
If only I knew then what I know now,
I would have held you a little longer,
kissed you a little stronger.
I would have found a way
to never let you leave me that day.
If only I knew that would be the last day,
I would have tried each & every last way,
to say how much I loved you,
how much I needed you,
how long I had dreamed of you & only you.

Honestly you were my truth
I'm living a lie without you.
I walk around pretending to be
the man that you wanted me to be,
but nothing feels as real as you.
Nothing fills the void you left
because nothing has your depth.
I miss you with every single breath.

Grieve

I'm not doing this right,
it just feels wrong,
how could you leave me here
to go through this all alone.
There's so much that I regret & I'm so upset
it's been months now &
the tears haven't stopped falling yet.
What comes next?
How do I move on?
I'm trying to hold it together
I'm trying to be strong,
but I feel weak inside,
how do I live without the one who taught me to survive?
This is suicide, in the slowest form
trying to live without you,
trying to carry on
I'm writing from my knees
asking God please
I just have one request,
send her back to me.

Strangers

How did you go
from being my whole world,
to just someone I used to know.
Strangers with a past
who are just hoping it doesn't show,
If I knew then
that in order to set you free
I'd have to let my world go
I'm not sure I could choose to lose you
knowing now what I know.

Prepared

Mentally I'm prepared,
I've planned for your departure,
it's okay if you leave,
but please
close the door to my heart behind you.
See, my mind is strong,
so I know what it can take,
but my heart is fragile,
so I know that it will break.
I'll pick up the pieces.
Eventually I'll mend.
Maybe one day in the future,
I'll attempt to love again.

Pretending

How long can we pretend
that love still lives here
in this empty residence.
There was a time when it seemed heaven-sent,
now regret looms in the air.
The only feeling that remains seems to be despair.
There's so much I want to say to you,
but we've drifted so far apart,
I wouldn't know where to start.
There used to be fire between us,
now there's not even a spark.

Silence

What happens when there's nothing left to say?
When you've tried all the different combinations of words
with ways that a message can be conveyed?
Even the stillness of this moment seems to fall on deaf
ears.
I don't recognize this place...
How did we get here?
In the midst of darkness & the absence of sound,
sometimes silence can be heard
when you don't focus on the words,
but you focus on the fact
that what was fact is now a lie,
and when lies unfold,
the only thing that remains
are unspoken words from broken hearts to broken souls.

Beyond

She was everything I needed
at a time when I had no clue what that was,
had no idea how to even ask God
for something like her.
Yet & still,
here she was.
She was something beyond beautiful,
a smile straight from heaven,
eyes that led to her soul & could see into mine.

To say, I loved her would be an understatement.
I adored her & she'll never know,
so many things I have to say
to ears that no longer hear.

A lifetime ago
we had a lifetime to go,
now a lifetime apart is all we'll ever know.

Hiding

How do you hide the fact that you still love someone?
A love that has no reason to still exist.
You try & hide these feelings within yourself,
desperately hoping that they don't escape.
I wonder if she can still see it in my eyes.
Does she hear the excitement in my voice
when I answer her call?
Subconsciously, do our souls still connect the same?
Are my efforts to hide in vain?
So many questions remain,
the answers to which I'm afraid to hear.
So, I'll ask these questions on this page
like whispers in the air,
the answers can remain.

Along with these feelings
I'm afraid to show,
while I wonder aloud
if she would even care to know.

Questions

Do you ever think about me?
Do you still hear my voice in your head
before you fall asleep?
Do I haunt your dreams
the way you haunt me
even when I'm awake?
It's 4 a.m.
I can't sleep.
I'm thinking of you,
wondering if you're thinking about me too.
Are we both fighting demons from the past?
Or am I battling alone & you're sound asleep
without a worry about me—
Just in case you are…
Sweet dreams.

Destiny

It wasn't you,
it wasn't me,
it was destiny.
You see, all the real love stories
are destined to be a tragedy,
bound to end tragically.

Sadly, we humans confuse emotions, lose focus,
consistently fall for the wrong traits & then lose faith.
Seems hopeless.
How much heartbreak can one soul take
before heartache becomes one's fate?
Maybe I'm misguided about the state of things,
overwhelmed from the weight of things,
undecided about what the future can bring.

If only I could unwind,
press rewind back to a time when…
It was you,
it was me,
it was destiny.

Writings on the Wall

The writings on the wall
I've seen it all before
the gift of premonition
seeing our future in my past.
Like the first love that didn't last
picture perfect
but only for a glance
although I hoped this time would be different.
I warned you
that this was how our story ended.

Maybe, I spoke this into existence,
or maybe this story was never meant to have a happy
ending.

Comfort Zone

You were comfortable with me.
After all, how could you not be comfortable?
With a man who is willing to give you his all
while expecting nothing.
You're not in love with me, but you love me
because I feel like home,
better yet, I make you feel at home
because I put you on a pedestal.
Treated you like a Queen, supported your dreams
while I whispered in your ear that you could do anything.
Your comfort zone was perfect
because it allowed you to receive
all the benefits of being loved

While maintaining your ability to roam
when things go wrong,
because after all,
we were never together; together,
we were just together alone.

8:21 a.m.

She said, "Eventually, I would truly break your heart."
I thought to myself,
thankfully
you can't break what you've already broken.

How Many

How many ways
can I write away the pain of yesterday?
How many poems
can I write to erase these tears?
How many words
can I say to prove that you made a mistake?
How many more to convince you to stay?
How many?
How many will it take?

Forgiveness

God forgives.
Although made in his image,
I am not him.
I don't forgive you & I won't pretend to.
There will be no amends.
You shattered my world into pieces...
HELL NO!
We can't be friends.
It's sad that after all these years,
this is how our story ends,
but I didn't write this ending...
I just closed the book.

Love & Hate

Love & hate
two opposite ends of a spectrum
one consumes you,
the other can doom you.
Here's the hitch,
you'll have to decide for yourself
which is which.

Ex

No matter how we left things
I could never regret you.
Although most days I did my best to forget you,
I know at times it seemed as if I hated you.
Truth is
at this moment, I thank you.
See you taught me things about myself,
I could've never learned on my own.
My instinct was to put others first,
in a relationship this can be a gift or a curse.
You were an example of everything I'll avoid,
because of you I was hardened,
I learned how to be guarded.

So, I should take this time to wish you well
but truthfully,
what I wish for you is…
Karma.

Karma

I didn't have any ill intentions,
I wasn't praying for your downfall,
I didn't notice you falling apart,
I was too busy rebuilding my broken parts.
I didn't wish you well, true,
but I never wished you harm.
The same energy that you gave to me,
it now seems someone has given you,
and this, my dear, is just how the universe moves.

Excuses

There's nothing you can tell me with words
to convince me you're different from the person,
you've shown yourself to be through actions.
People make excuses for doing,
what they've always wanted to do &
usually those excuses involve
putting the blame squarely on you.
Understand that no matter what you do,
It won't be enough.
If they cheat, it's your fault,
If they leave, it's your fault.
Either you didn't call enough,
Or you called too much.
Trust in the truth,
not the truth of your perspective,
but the truth that their actions
have more to do with them
than they do with you...

Fire

She was wild fire in the night.
The problem with fire is
as it burns bright
it's always looking for the next thing to ignite.
She was wrong for me, but I still tried to make her right.
Now she returns the favor
as a reason why I write.

Burning Bridges

Tonight I dance in the light of my newest friend
while my truth shines bright like the truest gem.
They weren't expecting this reaction.
It was new to them like a real name behind a pseudonym.
Hidden within my newfound strength.

Tonight I burn bridges
as if they were never meant to exist.

I'm burning bridges
for all those seeking my forgiveness as if it was a given.

I'm burning bridges
to all those who treated me like a doormat.
As if your apology would magically grant me
my wasted time back.

I'm burning bridges
to all those who disrespected
& then apologized as if it
were to be expected.

I'm burning bridges
to all those who betrayed, left me dismayed.

Tonight I burn bridges
& as the glare from the fire shines bright,
I hope you see me for the very last time
in a whole new light.

Withdrawn

I withdraw from the world at times.
The great escape into my mind,
living in my memories,
from time to time,
expressed by words drawn on pages.
From line to line.

I withdraw from the world…
Unsure if I do it to find myself or to hide myself.
Is this a form of depression or just my way of de-stressing?
It's just me.
Sometimes alone in my thoughts
is the only place where I can just be.
I know you don't understand.
Sometimes, I don't either, but every now & then

I need a breather.
Clarity or just a moment that matters to me,
tired of going through the motions,
hoping today is the day that I don't feel hopeless.

Turn the Page 2

Turn the page.
It just wasn't meant to be,
despite your best efforts,
you just couldn't make them see,
and that's okay.

Every failure isn't your fault.
A rejection isn't a reflection of something wrong with you,
you were never meant to live in your worst moments,
you were meant to move forward.

Turn the page,
your story is not over.

Alone

Alone in this loneliness
can't be what was meant for me.
I've scoured the universe
searching for the meaning of my broken dreams,
now it seems I've lost the only thing I had left:
Myself.
I'm in need of a life line
in the form of a like mind,
someone who understands
the pain of the pieces that remain after a world shatters,
when everything inside you screams,
nothing else in this world matters
when it all fades to black,
I need someone, something that can bring me back.

Poetry

Not sure if I found you
or you found me,
but here we are existing.
It took me awhile to open up to you,
at first I just listened as you explained my pain
like we were one & the same,
came to define me.

Now it seems I've been assigned to write
for those like minds,
wandering souls who are drawn to read,
may these words find you as they once found me.
You can take from them whatever you need—
The will to stand strong,
the strength to move on

Or just the knowledge that you're not lost alone.
I'll write to you directly
& you'll never have to interpret my words
because parts of me died so that they could be heard.

Melody

There's a melody when I write,
it's like writing the same love song over & over
from the perspective of every possible outcome,
an artist painting the same picture a thousand times
from a slightly different angle.

What you take from these portraits
will depend on the perspective
from where you're currently standing.
There's beauty in every story or love,
from the breathtaking to the heartbreaking
and all the stories in between.

Darkness

Late night rides to clear my mind
always seem to cloud my judgment.
I end up making decisions I live to regret,
like texting an ex & confessing my sins,
or professing my love of a dead situation to deaf ears,
on a dead end street.
It seems the dark of the night,
speaks to a certain darkness in me.
Much like the night it's always there,
it waits throughout my sunny days,
only to shine bright once the sun fades.

I just have to make it through tonight,
so I can live to regret another day.

Alcohol

Remembering my past times has become my pastime,
I take another shot & swear this will be the last time.
If it sounds familiar, it's probably because I said
the same thing the last time.
I drink too much & think too much and then
overthink all the thoughts that I was thinking of.
Finally my mind escapes to a place that knows no
time & space and I'm embraced by the emptiness
of every commitment made under the influence of alcohol.
Bad decisions and a lack of trust leads to acts of lust
and a morning full of regret.
Looking in the mirror wondering who
& what have I become.
I used to face my demons…
Now all I do is run.

Run

I run away,
sometimes from myself, sometimes giving chase.
I run from demons until I lose my way
and find myself in places where I cannot stay,
where I don't belong.
Over the years I've come to call these places home,
they say home is where the heart is,
what happens when home is also where the heart hurts,
where open wounds ensue.

I run away chasing after you.
A woman in need with my wounded heart on my sleeve,
if I could just give this to you,
surely you would know what to do.
After all you were in need & I was in pain & here I was,
thinking that we were the same,
but after you've taken everything that you need,
another wound ensues & I now find myself
running away from you.

Fear

Your fears are nothing
compared to your past
every obstacle seems small,
once you've found the strength to move pass.
That obstacle was once a giant,
back when you were running from it.
Now it seems so small,
seems like overcoming it shouldn't be an accomplishment
at all, but it is.
As will be your triumph over the next fear
whether it comes tomorrow or next year.
Fear can only survive in your mind,
the only failure you face comes from not trying.

Even

Even through my pain.
Even through my hurt.
Somehow, I still managed to put you first.
Gave you a position in my life
that you didn't deserve,
I still feel the pain of that choice with every word.
I'd run
if I could walk away
I'd leave
if my heart didn't yell STAY!!
I still hold on
even as you push me away.

IOYKHMILY

If I lived a thousand years, you would still be my
Only choice & I would still love
You in ways that I could never truly voice. You
Knew me before I knew myself. Look
How far we've come, look how
Much we've changed while remaining the same.
I love you as much now as I did that first day & that
Love will never fade. You may have doubts but if
You only knew the truth:

*The last line in this poem is all the bolded words read
from top to bottom*

Shame

Most of all I feel ashamed,
ashamed that after all this time,
you can still make me feel this way,
still leave me speechless,
when I have so much to say,
still counting the days until the next time I see your face,
still having a hard time
watching the future I saw in you fade away,
still loving the parts of you I miss
& missing the parts of you I love,
I'm hanging on by a thread
that's slowly unraveling.
I still love you,
but loving you is damaging.

The One

I remember the first time I looked into your eyes,
it caught me off guard,
I wasn't ready for the emotions that would follow,
but I knew this was different,
any thoughts of me instantly became we.
I stood there,
staring into your eyes & I thought to myself
that I could spend a lifetime in this moment
and it would be perfectly fine,
it would be a life well-spent,
it would be a life much like you
that I'd never forget,
as I sit here writing this I can't help getting upset…
You were the one

My one true love & losing you is my one true regret.
See, it's one thing to have a broken heart—
I've had that a time or two—
However, it's another thing entirely
when the mind breaks too.
Although my heart has healed,
mentally, I've never gotten over losing you.

Truth Be Told

I'm not strong enough to let go on my own; I need prayer'
I can't even pick up my phone because she's there.
She haunts my dreams & blesses my nightmares with her
presence being forever just out of my reach,
taunting me.
When love isn't enough, you're supposed to trust
that there's a love out there greater than the one
that's currently an absentee.
Made, designed & structured with the intent purpose
of being just for me.
At the moment I've misplaced my faith,
and what I used to believe has been replaced by cynicism,
which only furthers the division between
my heart & mind…
Only this time

I'm not sure both will survive.

Good Hearts

When you have a good heart
you have a guard it
as if your life depended on it
because it does.

I had to learn this
everyone doesn't deserve you,
and no matter how much you love them
some people haven't earned you,
your time, attention, love or trust.
Divorce yourself from this idea,
that if you just love them
a little bit more, for a little while longer,
suddenly it'll be enough.
That after you move heaven & earth
finally they'll see your worth.
It won't work.

Save yourself the heartache,
because good hearts are always the first to break.

Alive

When a heart breaks,
the door to that heart can seal
concealing all the pain, resentment & bitterness within,
no love can survive here.
What happens when a heart cries?
After all the second chances, the makeups to breakups,
all the hellos & the final goodbye.
This moment is the place where love goes to die.
When there's nothing left to try or hold onto
you let go of all emotion &
you question the reasons behind everything from your
decisions to your existence.
Even as the answers continue to elude you,
the tightness in your chest will eventually subdue &
every breath will feel brand new.
You'll survive the sleepless nights & the memories will no
longer make you cry.
Despite thinking, you couldn't live without them
you'll find yourself, very much…
Alive.

This is what happens when a broken heart heals.

Break To Build

The heart has a unique ability
to withstand being broken multiple times,
while each time, rebuilding itself
stronger than it was before.
Anything broken can heal, & yes, that includes you.
I know you still love them, but tell me something:
Do you still love you?
Healing starts with small steps,
maybe just one or two.
So, for today
instead of choosing them, simply choose you.

Heal

What comes after the pain?
After the trauma of being hurt,
how do you heal after a loss?
How do you find your way back
after losing yourself?
You've tried it all.
You shut down every emotion you could feel
in an effort to heal but it wasn't real,
it didn't work because it wasn't you,
you could never be someone else
nor could you pretend to be.
The truth has always been within you.

Love is your true destiny.
Every heartache, heartbreak,
all the cheating, the lies, the half-truths,
the verbal & mental abuse
have led you to this moment.
Here you stand unbroken
despite all that you've been through.
You still have the capacity to love,
you still yearn to feel something unconditional,
you've bottled up everything you have inside you,
patiently waiting on someone special,
never realizing that someone special
has been here all along…
All the love you've waited so long
to give to someone else, you must give to yourself.
The only way to truly heal is to unconditionally
LOVE YOURSELF.

God's Plan

Sometimes the love you dream of
has been awake in your life for years,
but you couldn't see pass the package it arrived in.
We spend so much time searching for the right one,
we ignore the ones right in front of us,
we ignore their unquestioned trust,
we ignore their unconditional love,
we ignore everything in them we say we need from love,
all in search of more; more of what we want.
The difference between wants & needs
is the difference between God's plan and your plan.
What you want,
may not always be what you need,
and what you need

May not come in a package that initially appeals to the eye.
When God wants to speak to you,
guide you,
lead you,
he doesn't reveal himself to the eye,
he reveals himself to the heart.
Open eyes with perfect sight & a closed heart
are still blind to the wonders of the world,
so when someone comes into your life,
instead of wondering whether they're wrong or right,
question whether they appeal to the eye superficially
or if they spoke to your heart initially.

Choose YOU 2

I know you're tired &
you feel like giving up.
You don't know which way to go &
you feel stuck,
in a never-ending cycle of
broken hearts & broken trust.
You're tired of being alone &
tired of putting yourself out there,
only to be met with disappointment.
Every time you think you've found the right one
you're always proven wrong,
and if it feels like these words hit home.

I know your story
because it is my own.

So, sit back & relax
just for a minute,
close your eyes
and imagine yourself receiving
all the love that you've so freely given,
to those that didn't deserve you.
Imagine how being loved this way
could change your entire world view.
Now open your eyes & realize,
the love you just imagined resides within you,
and you have the power
to decide who you give it to.
There's literally no one who deserves your love

More than you do…

Choose you.

Blessed

Blessed are those who can learn the lessons.
Who know enough to know,
that they don't know everything,
and can still change perspectives.

Thankful

Thankful for it all.
The good & the bad...
I found the blessings in it all,
even when I failed.
The lesson was in the fall,
I went from questioning
to giving my testament,
I had to lose it all twice,
to find out how blessed I've been,
there was no accident,
everything was heaven-sent,
I'm exactly where I'm supposed to be
and I have everything that's meant for me,
so I'm thankful for today

Because, I know that it was meant to be.

Outro

You can't see my scars,
I've disguised them well.

You can't see my journey,
but I've been through hell.

You can't see my tears,
I only cry in the rain.

You can't see my hurt,
I conceal my pain.

You can't see my truth,
it's hidden in shame.

You can't see the real me,
because I'm not who I used to be.

That person is dead,
the only thing left are the words he never said.

ABOUT THE AUTHOR

MPJ is an up-and-coming poet born & raised in Baton Rouge, Louisiana. He began writing poetry in his teenage years, and has continued into adulthood. He has always been a person who searches for the deeper meaning in everything, from music to relationships to life in general. He uses his writing to tell stories, share memories, or express his thoughts and feelings on a specific topic or moment in time. In addition to his writing, his love of technology and more specifically computers drew him to become an information technology major in college, a field in which he works to this day.

For more information about the author you can follow him on:
Instagram: @PoemsbyMPJ
Twitter: PoemsbyMP
Facebook: MPJ